# Making Sense of SQL

# Making Sense of SQL

**Steve Thomas**

2014

First Printing: 2014

ISBN 978-1-312-54553-3

# Contents

Acknowledgements..................................................................vi

Preface ...............................................................................vii

Introduction .........................................................................1

The Database........................................................................3

Relationships .......................................................................6

Normalization ......................................................................8

Tables................................................................................11

Parts of a SQL query ..........................................................13

JOINS (small, but important, digression) ............................16

Parts of a SQL query (continued)........................................19

Where Did It All Go Wrong?................................................28

Troubleshooting..................................................................32

Style ..................................................................................33

Odds and Ends....................................................................36

# Acknowledgements

I would like to thank my wife, Lynne, my son, Quentin, and my friends and colleagues, Meary Barbeau and Neil Shepherd, for their suggestions. Lynne and Quentin have been waiting patiently for this book so that they might have some idea about what I have been talking about for many years. They were also helpful with their questions, observations, and proofreading. Meary managed Level 1 support and asked for a short, simple book about SQL which, in many ways, kick-started this book. Neil is a programmer of long standing with a flair for keeping the simple simple and only complicating when absolutely necessary.

This book is more useful because of them.

# Preface

Many years ago one of my English professors walked into the classroom on the first day, set his briefcase on the desk, walked to the far end of the chalkboard(!), and wrote "WIAM" in large letters. Then he walked to the other end of the board and wrote "ODTAA." He then sat on the edge of the desk and stared at his mystified class.

Finally, he gestured to his right. "WIAM," he said. "What It All Means." He gestured to his left. "ODTAA," he said. "One Darn Thing After Another."

He gestured back towards WIAM. "Give me this."

He pointed directly at ODTAA. "Do not give me that!"

This is my WIAM about SQL.

# Introduction

Structured Query Language (SQL) is the language used to SELECT, UPDATE, INSERT, and DELETE data in a relational database management system (RDBMS), or just database for short. The purpose of this book is to provide a framework for understanding how a database is designed and how it works, and to give a basic understanding of how and why to join tables to get back the results that you need.

This book is my attempt to distill the answers to common questions that I have answered over the years in various development and reporting environments. The intended audience is the casual user of SQL, such as people who are in a support or a part-time reporting role. Rather than focusing on the syntax of SQL, which varies between "flavors" of databases, this book will explain why things are the way they are in a database, and how to get the data that you want.

As mentioned above, it is important to realize at the outset that the syntax varies between database vendors. SQL Server syntax is not exactly the same as Oracle syntax. Those, in turn, are not exactly the same as MySQL syntax. There are international standards for SQL, but no vendor is completely compliant. The big point to take away is that a given SQL statement might not be completely portable between different database vendors.

A second and more subtle point that can be made is that no SQL implementation is "the best." Every user has to learn the nuances of a new SQL flavor when working with a new database vendor. Often, "better" is just a way of saying "more familiar."

One other common complaint which should probably be addressed here is the notion that "the database hates me." This probably better stated as "the database does not understand me." There is no easy fix for this, as the list of possible causes of misunderstanding might range from a simple syntax error to a completely unintelligible SQL statement. The database itself is completely indifferent to you as a user. The same cannot always be said for the database administrator (DBA) who is responsible for that particular database!

# The Database

Let's take a moment to step back from SQL look at what makes up a relational database. A database is made up of one or more tables. In a well-designed database, the tables will be "related." What exactly does that mean?

The essence of a relational database is that data should be stored once and referenced many times. Huh?! To understand this idea, it is necessary to drill down further and look at what makes a table and why good design is so important.

A database table is the implementation of a single conceptual entity. More simply put, a table named BOOKS should be about books, and only about books. Every field in that table should support the general notion of books. What fields would be used to store data about a book? For starters, items such as ISBN, title, author, publisher, and genre spring to mind. Each of those is an important descriptor and/or classifier of a given book.

This leads to another very important relational characteristic. Each row in a table should have a unique identifier, also known as a primary key. This unique identifier can be as simple as the next number in a sequence. The unique identifier can also be a compound key, which combines two or more table fields in a specified order.

The unique identifier can be a natural key or a surrogate key. The ISBN, or International Standard Book Number, reference above is an example of a natural key, which is a value which uniquely identifies an entity, in this case, a book, and already exists in the outside world. A surrogate key, by contrast, only lives in a specific database. Often the surrogate key is a sequence. Since the sequence is specific to a single table in a single database, that value has no relevance or reference in other databases. It is just a surrogate, or "stand in", as a unique value to identify a row in the table.

Returning to the conceptual BOOKS table, then, the ISBN might or might not be a good choice for a unique key. If all of the books in the database have an ISBN number, then that might be good choice for a unique key. If you need to catalog any books that do not have an ISBN number now or in the future, then the ISBN number is not a good candidate for the unique identifier. I mention this because every design decision is made with some assumptions. Some of these assumptions hold up "forever" (forever is not over yet!) and some require some re-architecting of tables which can nullify some earlier SQL that you wrote.

Some might consider a compound key of, say, title and author. That should be unique presuming that a given author does not give two different publications the same title! The disadvantages are that the key becomes relatively long, it is prone to spelling/spacing/capitalization errors, and difficult to keep in sync with related tables should the author choose to change his or her name.

For this example, let us just decide to use a sequence and put in a field named BOOK_ID. That satisfies the uniqueness criteria for each row in the table. At this point, you might start entering data in the table. Let us assume that you are entering data from a list. As you check back in the database to see your progress, you might notice one or more author appearing in several records.

You are now looking at what might become your first database relationship! Entering the author's name twice might not be a big deal, but what if it is a very prolific author? Is every database entry EXACTLY the same for each instance of the author's name? Are there extra spaces anywhere? Did you not capitalize a first or last name once? Did you enter a period after the middle initial on all of the records? All of these questions hearken back to the essential idea of "store once and reference many times."

Why do you care and what does it matter? Since the table is BOOKS, let us use the example of Georges Joseph Christian Simenon, author of some 200 novels. Consider how many spelling, misspelling, spacing, and capitalization permutations are available. If the full name is entered every time, I can guarantee that several of these permutations will make their way into the database. The problem comes about during retrieval. If you search for "Georges Simenon", you will retrieve records with that author name, but not the record with, say, "George Simenon" in the author field.

Conceptually, rather than adding every permutation of the name to your search, the solution might be to create a separate AUTHORS table. This table might have fields such as AUTHOR_ID (per the discussion above), name, date of birth, and date of death. Not every field requires a value for every row, so the date of death field could be left blank for living authors. In the sad event of an author's demise, the date of death need only be filled in once, in the AUTHORS table.

Having created and populated an AUTHORS table, you would then replace the AUTHOR_NAME field in the BOOKS table with an AUTHOR_ID field. Each row in the BOOKS table would have to be updated with the correct AUTHOR_ID, and then the AUTHOR_NAME field would be dropped. Congratulations! You now have your first database relationship!

# Relationships

The above discussion showed a conceptual process of how tables get related during a design phase. There are some SQL commands that must be run in addition to just adding the field to formalize the relationship between the "parent" key, in this case the AUTHOR_ID field in the AUTHORS table, and the "child" key, in this case the AUTHOR_ID field in the BOOKS table. This is an important point because record relationships in a relational database are treated differently than non-related records.

In the parent table, in this case AUTHORS, the AUTHOR_ID field must be designated via SQL as a primary key. Designating a field as a primary key tells the database that the values in that field must be unique, that the database needs to create a UNIQUE index to enforce the field's uniqueness, and makes that field eligible for "foreign key" fields in other tables to reference the primary key values.

It is this key relationship that satisfies the "store once, reference many times" requirement. Now the name of the author, and any other additional information about the author, is stored in the AUTHOR table. Once. The information about that author can be referenced many times by inserting the unique AUTHOR_ID in another table. Joining the two tables using the AUTHOR_ID parent-child relational key gives access to the other fields in the AUTHOR table.

One point that might be a little confusing given the "parent-child" terminology is that the primary key value – the "parent" – is not required to have a foreign key in another table – the "child" - related to it. In other words, a primary key is only a "parent" when it has a "child". A primary key that is not referenced by a foreign key is just a unique value. Going back to the example, this can happen if your database includes only books that you own. If you dispose of the only book that you own by a particular author, you can remove the record in the BOOKS table, but you would probably want to keep that author row in the AUTHORS table in the chance that you acquire another book by that author. In that case, the reference value (AUTHOR_ID) already exists in the database. The flip side is that one primary key value can be referenced many times. Obviously, an author can write more than one book.

This brings up another point with respect to relationships. When a primary key – foreign key relationship is set up, it can be set up with or without a CASCADE DELETE (or similar terminology depending on the RDBMS vendor). In a CASCADE DELETE relationship, when the primary key value is deleted (actually the entire row identified by the primary key value is deleted), the database will automatically trace all of the CASCADE DELETE foreign keys that reference that primary key value and it will delete them as well. The CASCADE DELETE is a very clinical way of saying "I will get rid of you and all of your children!" Note that this delete only works from the parent down (CASCADE). While this seems pretty handy, it can be dangerous. Using the example, if you delete an author, the database will report something like "1 row deleted" which is what you would expect. What if you actually did have a book by that author? That row would disappear from the BOOKS table without a warning or even a notification. This is an example of where knowing details about a database can save you from a very painful discussion with the owner of the database.

In the absence of CASCADE DELETE, the primary key cannot be deleted as long as child records exist. This prevents the orphaning of child rows. Using the example, no author referenced in the BOOKS table could be deleted unless the referenced rows in the BOOKS table were deleted first. This protection ensures that every book has an author during data retrieval.

While relationships may seem a little convoluted at first glance, the thinking behind them is very practical. To get a little more insight, let's take a moment to look at normalization.

# Normalization

The process of making a database relational is called normalization. There are codified rules, also called normal forms, several of which are very directly concerned with tables specifically. The exact definitions can be a bit difficult to understand, but they can be paraphrased as:

- Each field contains the smallest data element possible

- Each field only contains one data item

- Each record must be unique

- No entry should be repeated

- Each field supports the primary key and only the primary key

Let's take a moment to understand these points.

- Each field contains the smallest data element possible

This is a precautionary requirement that is a corollary of the statement, "junk will accumulate to fill available space." As a practical matter, the smaller a field is, the easier it is to index and search, and the smaller the chance for error during data entry. Note that this does not place any arbitrary limits on the size of a field; rather, it obliquely requires the database designer to give the matter of each field in each table some thought. Not a bad thing.

- Each field only contains one data item

The idea here is to avoid having a "miscellaneous" field. It also means that a field should not contain comma separated lists, for example. A multivalued list inherently sounds like a related table waiting to happen, and probably should be!

- Each record must be unique

This is the heart of the relational database concept. If a record is unique, knowing the key value gives the user access to all of the related data in that row. In the absence of uniqueness, the table becomes a sort of junk drawer, requiring a lot more effort to retrieve and utilize the data it contains.

- No entry should be repeated

While this sounds like a repetition of the previous requirement, it is not. Remember the idea of using a sequence to create a unique identifier? That is a pretty elegant idea, except that it has nothing to do with the data in the table. It is just a number. Unfortunately, this means that the same data can be entered in the other fields repeatedly. The unique identifier makes the row, as a whole, unique! Think of this as a cautionary reminder that no solution is perfect!

- Each field supports the primary key and only the primary key

This is the requirement that conceptually forces the idea of related tables. Consider the original idea of the BOOKS table, which included the author name. Remember that in the original concept the book title was the "primary key". Therefore, including the author name makes sense, because every book needs to have an author, so that field supports the primary key. However, including the author name would not satisfy the "only the primary key" part. Having a second book by the same author would mean that the author now supports two primary keys (books). At this point, the rules of normalization would require that the author be split out into a related table.

As you can see, just normalizing using even this subset of the normal forms can lead to some headaches. You should also be able to see where the notion of relating tables makes quite a bit of sense. Using the example, breaking out author information in to a separate AUTHORS table makes adding fields about authors fairly trivial. If the author data is included in the BOOKS table, it becomes much more cumbersome to keep all of the author data correct and in synch as changes occur. In addition, adding a field such as DOB (date of birth) to the BOOKS table does not conceptually make sense as the author's birthday has nothing to with the book itself.

# Tables

By now, you should have a feel for the importance of good design in the database in general, and in tables specifically. The "goodness" of the design will ultimately help to determine the level of difficulty you will encounter when writing SQL statements to manipulate data in the database.

There is another important factor in table design which affects the SQL that you will write, and that is datatypes. In most modern RDBMS systems, there are four basic datatypes (and examples):

- Character (CHAR, VARCHAR, VARCHAR2, NCHAR, NVARCHAR2)

- Number (NUMBER, FLOAT, INTEGER)

- Datetime (DATE, TIMESTAMP)

- Binary (LOB, CLOB, NCLOB, BFILE)

Within those four basic datatypes, there may be subcategories and datatype subsets unique to each vendor, as the examples in parentheses indicate. In general, however, these four general descriptors encompass most, if not all, of the available datatypes.

The underlying issue is that, ultimately, there are effectively two types of data: character and binary. The character dataset includes all alphanumeric characters, so a number can be stored in a character field. Likewise, datetime data is ultimately numeric (number of days since some reference date, including a decimal representation of the fractions of the day) and can be stored in a character field as well. Binary data is treated differently depending on the vendor implementation, but generally includes some sort of "pointer" value and then the binary data itself stored at the "pointer" location.

In a database, unlike, for instance, a spreadsheet, the data is actually stored as the specified datatype and is validated as being that datatype prior to the data being inserted into the table. In a spreadsheet, for example, a column can be formatted as "number", but there is no default method that automatically checks incoming values and prevents a user from entering, say, "Bob" into that column. In a database, by contrast, every value entered is checked prior to be committed to the database. Non-numeric values cannot be stored in a field with a datatype of NUMBER.

Another common example involves storing dates as character data. Any character value can be inserted with no inherent validation as to whether the inserted value is a real date. This anomaly is often found when subsequent SQL is run to, for instance, find all rows with a date that is prior to a given date (WHERE <date field> < TO_DATE('06/08/2012','MM/DD/YYYY')). Now the database is forced to read the data in the character field, test that the data represents a valid date, and then compare it to the given date. An entry such as "Bob" will cause the database to throw up an error indicating that it could not make a date value out of some data, generally not even referencing the row(s) with bad data. Now someone has to track down which row has bad data and figure out what the correct date should be. It is so much easier to have the database validate the entry at the time of data entry than to try to track that same data down later.

In a nutshell, the best design stores binary data as a binary datatype, dates as a date datatype, numbers as a numeric datatype, and character data as a character datatype. Doing so harnesses the unseen, but powerful, datatype checking that is available in a database.

Now, with a very basic understanding of the database environment, we can return to the discussion of SQL!

# Parts of a SQL query

The "structured" part of SQL has to be extremely structured. Why? Every user in every country must use the same language to query their database, regardless of the syntactic conventions of their native language. While that might make for a seemingly "clunky" language, the fact that it is so structured makes it much easier to learn the basics. This book will focus on the SELECT operation for several reasons as it is the most common operation, and the one most often performed by casual SQL users.

Although the examples will often show SQL key words (called "reserved words") such as SELECT and FROM in capital letters, the capitalization is not required. SQL text is case-insensitive. There will be more about this later in a Style section!

Breaking it down into sections, or clauses, there are potentially five parts to a SQL statement:

- SELECT

- FROM

- WHERE

- GROUP BY

- ORDER BY

The first two parts (SELECT, FROM) are required, and the last three are optional, depending on the query and your coding style. That's it! That being said, these parts can be combined in many and varied ways to do magical things, but we will leave that for another day.

## SELECT

The SELECT keyword is followed by the comma-separated list of fields from the database that you want to retrieve.

```
SELECT title
    , page_count
    , publisher
    , first_edition_year
FROM books;
```

The SELECT clause is also where you would apply any transformations or perform any operations that you want to see in your final output. Every current RDBMS platform has a fair number of available operations that it can perform. The possible operations range from simple math to regular expressions to text manipulation to if/then structures. The possibilities are virtually limitless. The best place for finding out what is available is to check the documentation from your database vendor. The real difficulty is often finding out the name of your desired function, particularly when switching between database vendors. Sometimes there is just no substitute for reading through a lot of documentation.

There will more about this in the Style chapter. Stay tuned.

## FROM

The FROM clause signifies the end of a SELECT clause and contains the names of the tables from which you are selecting data. There are some important nuances here that might require some explanation.

The first nuance is the syntax for joining tables. The older syntax for joining tables just lists the names of the tables in the query, separated by commas, and perhaps aliases for the tables, as in:

```
FROM books b
    , authors a
```

The table names in this example are BOOKS and AUTHORS. The "b" and "a" are aliases for the BOOKS and AUTHORS tables, respectively. Aliasing the tables allows you to refer to columns in the BOOKS table, for example, as b.<column_name>, rather than as books.<column_name>. It can be a handy feature, particularly if you have one or more tables with very long names!

The older syntax lists the table names in the FROM clause and puts the join condition(s) in the WHERE clause. There is a certain logical purity with putting only FROM items, typically tables, in the FROM clause. A complete join example, using the traditional syntax, would then look like:

```
FROM books b
   , authors a
 WHERE b.author_id = a.author_id
```

This joins the two tables using the author_id field. One of the oddities that you might encounter when using this syntax is that if you SELECT the author_id field without prepending an alias or table name to the field, the database will require you to do so, even though the value will be the same for either table since the join is where the two values are equal!

The newer syntax includes the join condition in the FROM clause, as in:

```
 FROM books JOIN authors USING (author_id)
```

Conceptually, this syntax reserves the WHERE clause for additional criteria apart from the actual joining of the tables. In practice, there should be no difference between the two as they accomplish the same work using two different syntaxes.

## JOINS (small, but important, digression)

Joining tables is sometimes confusing for people, particularly when they do not understand the options that are available. There are four types of joins: equi-join, left outer join, right outer join, and full outer join.

Remember that the primary key for table A is a placeholder when it is a foreign key in any other table. For example, by joining the BOOKS table and the AUTHORS table using the AUTHOR_ID field, one can reference fields in both tables:

```
SELECT a.name
  , a.birth_date
  , b.title
  , b.page_count
  , b.publisher
FROM books b
  , authors a
WHERE b.author_id = a.author_id
  AND a.authorid = 1;
```

As you can see, two fields have been selected from the AUTHORS table, and three fields from the BOOKS table. It is also important to note that the join field (AUTHOR_ID) is not required to be one of the fields in the SELECT clause. It certainly can be part of the SELECT clause, but it can also just serve as a JOIN condition.

### EQUI-JOIN (=, JOIN, INNER JOIN)

The equi-join is the most common join and the simplest to explain. This is just a pure equality between the joining fields in each table. If the value does not exist in one or the other table, that row is not included in the final output. Thinking about it in parent-child terms, if there is not a child record, the parent record will not be selected. The traditional FROM syntax would couple with the equals sign (=), while the newer syntax would make use of either the JOIN or INNER JOIN keywords.

## LEFT OUTER JOIN ((+), LEFT JOIN)

This join is very literal and visual, following the order of the tables in the WHERE or FROM clause. This type of join means "give me all of the rows from the table on the left and only the matching rows from the table on the right." All of the rows returned would also be subject to any other conditions imposed by the WHERE clause, but the idea is that you want all of the records from one table whether they match or not, and only matching values from the other table. The non-matching rows from the "right-side" table will have NULL values returned in each field selected from that table.

The left outer join (or the right outer join covered next) is most often used when you need to find the absence of something. The SQL includes a "WHERE <right_table>.<join_field> IS NULL" clause which makes use of the fact that the database returns a NULL value for the "absent" field. An example would be if you wanted to find authors who had no books in your collection:

```
SELECT a.author_id
FROM authors a LEFT OUTER JOIN books b USING
(author_id)
WHERE b.author_id IS NULL
```

All of the records from AUTHOR are returned, minus the rows where the author_id matches one or more rows in the BOOKS table.

The old syntax for an outer join in Oracle was quite obscure. It looked like:

```
SELECT a.author_id
FROM authors a
, books b
WHERE a.author_id = b.author_id (+)
AND b.author_id IS NULL
```

To this day I still have to pause for a moment to confirm which table is the outer join. My best memory aid is to think of the above example as "where a.author_id equals b.author_id PLUS NULLS and b.author_id is NULL." The newer syntax makes the relationship so much clearer!

## RIGHT OUTER JOIN ((+), RIGHT JOIN)

This is the same as the previous join, only trying to find entries in the right-hand table that do not have entries in the left-hand table. Again, this type of join is most often used to find "absent" values. If the previous "new" syntax query was written with RIGHT OUTER JOIN, it would look like:

```
SELECT a.author_id
FROM authors a RIGHT OUTER JOIN books b
USING (author_id)
WHERE a.author_id IS NULL
```

Conceptually, this is "find all of the books that do not have a matching author." Thinking back to the whole relationship discussion earlier, you might wonder how this could happen. The potential causes are beyond the scope of this book, but might include accidentally dropping a foreign key or perhaps not creating a formal key relationship and the two tables got out of sync.

## FULL OUTER JOIN (FULL JOIN)

This is quite literally "give me every row from both tables whether the join matches or not." This one is a head-scratcher from a use-case point of view. It is conceivable that you might be looking at a database that did not have formal relationships set up between the tables and you are trying to get a sense of how badly mismatched the data has become. The sheer amount of data might quickly get overwhelming in that situation, however. It would probably be preferable to find orphaned records on each side of the join separately and then verify the quality of the equi-joined data in three separate steps rather than try to get everything in one pass.

# Parts of a SQL query (continued)

The two other basic, but optional (sometimes!), parts of a SQL statement are the WHERE and GROUP BY clauses. The WHERE clause is almost always used, unless you are just running a "dump" query to get everything from one or more tables. The GROUP BY clause is required in some situations and it is not particularly well understood by the average user. Well, not yet.

## WHERE

In addition to holding the joins in the traditional syntax, the WHERE clause is the place where conditions are imposed to specify what data is to be returned. Simply put, this is where you include and exclude data. Typically, a query will include one or more comparison conditions such as equals (=), greater than (>), less than (<), or a greater/less than or equal to condition (<=, >=). Putting an exclamation point in front of the equal sign (!=) negates the "equal" and makes it a "not equal".

There is no realistic limit to the number of conditions that can be added to a WHERE clause. The word "realistic" is used because, even though the database may be able to handle them, having a huge number of WHERE conditions often indicates that you are running a not particularly well thought out query. There will be more about this in the "Where Did It All Go Wrong" section later.

There are also several operators that can be used to join all of the WHERE conditions. The two most common are AND and OR. The AND conditions act just as you would expect if you were asking for something with several conditions, such as "I would like a room that has two beds, a view of the pool, and costs $200 or less." Conceptually, this might look like:

```
SELECT room_id
FROM rooms
WHERE beds = 2
```

```
AND overlooks = 'POOL'
AND rate <= 200
```

The WHERE clause can get a little messier when using the OR operator, as in "I would like a room that is $200 or less and has two beds or a view of the pool." Now this may sound pedantic, but this is actually an ambiguous request!

```
SELECT room_id
FROM rooms
WHERE beds = 2
  AND overlooks = 'POOL'
  OR rate <= 200
```

This example query would return all rooms costing $200 or less regardless of the number of beds or the view as well as 2-bed rooms overlooking the pool that cost more than $200! Why is that?

The simple answer is "perception". A human might likely perceive the request "I would like a room that is $200 or less and has two beds or a view of the pool" as "I would like a room that costs $200 or less. I would like it to have either two beds or a view of the pool." That would be the contextual "I know what you meant even though that is not EXACTLY what you said" filter that people often use.

A database is entirely literal and has no contextual understanding. The database sees three separate conditions and will tend to apply them left to right (top to bottom). This is not guaranteed behavior, so do not rely on it! Assuming a top to bottom application, the top two conditions would be implicitly grouped together (AND), and the last condition would be the "other" option (OR). Therefore, a $100, 3-bed room facing the parking lot would not meet the first two conditions, but would be returned by the database because it satisfies the "rate <= 200" OR condition.

The solution, when using OR conditions, is to put parentheses around the OR conditions. Just as in math, this groups the OR conditions and separates them from any other individual or grouped conditions.

Using the example, the WHERE clause could be unambiguously restated as:

```
WHERE beds = 2
    AND (overlooks = 'POOL'
    OR rate <= 200)
```

"Two beds.  Room can either overlook the pool or cost $200 or less."

Or:

```
WHERE (beds = 2
    AND overlooks = 'POOL')
    OR rate <= 200
```

"Two beds and overlooks the pool or else it must cost $200 or less."

There are some additional things to know when searching textual data.  The most important is to surround the search term with single quotes.  Negating a textual "equals" condition can be written as either "!=" or as "<>".  It is common to see either usage.

The WHERE conditions for textual data are not limited to exact comparisons.  The language allows for a wildcard search.  The wildcard character is typically a percent sign (%).  The key difference in the syntax is that the wildcard condition has to be (NOT) LIKE rather than "=", as in:

```
WHERE name LIKE 'Bob%'
```

This LIKE condition would find "Bob", "Bobaloo", and "Bobby". The use of wildcards in the textual search is not limited to the end of search term.  The wildcard can appear anywhere in the term, and may even be used more than once in the same search condition!  Keep in mind, though, that wildcard searches, particularly those that have the wildcards at the front of the search condition, generally take a bit longer as they typically have to traverse all of the records in the table and search the entirety of the field in question to verify that that record satisfies or does not satisfy the wildcard condition.

When matching textual data, your database may perform a case-sensitive match. In those cases, searching for "Bob" will not match "BOB" or "bob". There are a few different methods for "simulating" a case-insensitive match, such as using the UPPER function to read the data in upper-case and compare it your upper-cased search value, but most – if not all! – of the methods involving changing case are slower than exact case matches.

# GROUP BY

The GROUP BY clause is used when the data is being aggregated using a function such as COUNT, MIN, or MAX. However, if you are only selecting an aggregated value such as a COUNT, MIN, or MAX, there is no need for a GROUP BY clause.

```
SELECT COUNT(*)
FROM books;
```

If you think about it, this mirrors real life. If you are asked to count the number of items on a list, for example, there is no need for grouping. There is no need for grouping even when there is a condition, such as "count the items in red." It is only when you need to aggregate into, well, groups that you need a GROUP BY clause. An example of this would be "How many people are in this room by gender?"

Here is a small example. Here is a table with four fields (ID, NAME, GENDER, BIRTH_DATE) and five rows of data:

```
ID NAME       G BIRTH_DAT
--- ---------- - ---------
  1 Gru        M 31-OCT-66
  2 Margo      F 04-JUN-00
  3 Edith      F 17-AUG-02
  4 Agnes      F 03-MAR-06
```

```
5 Ms Hattie  F 22-NOV-75
```

Now, the query "How many people are there by gender?" would look like:

```
SELECT gender
   , COUNT(*) as ct
FROM people
GROUP BY gender;

G          CT
- ----------
M           1
F           4
```

The GROUP BY clause gets a little more confusing when several fields are selected and there is an aggregate function used. Every field that is not part of the aggregation must be listed in the GROUP BY clause. Remember how the database is perfectly literal and makes no assumptions? Logically, the above SQL without the GROUP BY clause could be considered to be "select the gender and gender count of everyone in the people table." This would return every row and would list the gender and a count of 1, because every row has exactly one gender column. That is not typically what you want and, actually, the database will not let you do it!

There is also no limit to the number of aggregate functions that can be used in a statement. Consider a question like "What is the count by gender in the PEOPLE table and what is the age spread by gender?" This would look like:

```
SELECT gender
   , COUNT(*) as ct
   , MIN(birth_date) as oldest
   , MAX(birth_date) as youngest
FROM people
GROUP BY gender;
```

| G | CT | OLDEST | YOUNGEST |
| - | ---------- | --------- | --------- |
| M | 1 | 31-OCT-66 | 31-OCT-66 |
| F | 4 | 22-NOV-75 | 03-MAR-06 |

Notice that in this example, the minimum and maximum BIRTH_DATE are shown for each gender, as well as the count. Since gender is not being aggregated, it must be included in the GROUP BY clause. Because the MIN and MAX built-in aggregation functions are being applied to the BIRTH_DATE field, that field is not part of the GROUP BY clause.

The GROUP BY clause probably causes the most angst among SQL writers. A common mistake is to just add every field in the SELECT statement to the GROUP BY clause, as in:

```
SELECT gender
  , COUNT(*) as ct
  , MIN(birth_date) as oldest
  , MAX(birth_date) as youngest
FROM people
GROUP BY gender
  , birth_date;
```

| G | CT | OLDEST | YOUNGEST |
| - | ---------- | --------- | --------- |
| F | 1 | 04-JUN-00 | 04-JUN-00 |
| F | 1 | 03-MAR-06 | 03-MAR-06 |
| F | 1 | 22-NOV-75 | 22-NOV-75 |
| M | 1 | 31-OCT-66 | 31-OCT-66 |
| F | 1 | 17-AUG-02 | 17-AUG-02 |

By adding the aggregated column BIRTH_DATE to the GROUP BY clause, you have changed the question to be "What is the count by gender *and birth date* in the PEOPLE table and what is the age spread by gender *and birth date*?"

Sometimes it is helpful to just remove yourself from the SQL and just focus on the question that you want to ask. "By gender, how many rows are in the PEOPLE table and what is the minimum and maximum birth date?" The "by gender" is the GROUP BY clause!

## HAVING

The HAVING clause is less familiar to most users, but it can be extremely useful. The HAVING clause can only follow a GROUP BY clause as it is a conditional clause for an aggregate function. This clause is used to find groupings that meet the HAVING condition.

For instance, say that you are tasked with finding all products in a warehouse that have fewer than three examples in stock. One approach would be to list out a count by product and visually skim the list to find counts less than three. Obviously, this would be tedious for a large warehouse. This becomes easy with the HAVING clause:

```
SELECT product_id
  , COUNT(*)
FROM products
GROUP BY product_id
HAVING COUNT(*) < 3
```

It is important to know that the HAVING clause comes into play *after* the GROUP BY clause is applied. The HAVING clause is really for removing post-aggregate rows that are not of interest. It may be confusing at first, but after GROUP BY clauses become comfortable for you, there will be a "Ding!" moment when you realize where the HAVING clause may be useful.

## ORDER BY

The ORDER BY clause is used to sort the returned rows by one or more column values. Most importantly, the ORDER BY clause is the only way to guarantee the order of the returned rows. If there is a requirement that the rows be returned in a particular order, then an ORDER BY clause must be used.

Any number of columns can be used for sorting, and the sort can either be ascending (ASC), which is the default, or descending (DESC). Furthermore, the sort is done by column, so mixing and matching ascending and descending sorts is possible.

```
SELECT title
    , page_count
    , publisher
    , first_edition_year
FROM books
ORDER BY first_edition_year DESC;
```

This SQL will list books in a descending order by first_edition_year. Something to watch for is that this statement, as written, will not always return rows in the same order! But I thought you said...? Since many new books are published each year, it is likely that this table of books will contain several books which had their first editions published in the same year. Therefore, the first_edition_year will be sorted in the correct (descending) order, but the other three fields might not always be returned in the same order. To ensure that the results come back in the same order, it would be necessary to add additional columns to the ORDER BY clause.

One other note is that the ORDER BY syntax includes support for referencing columns by their order in the SELECT statement, the first column selected being 1, the second is 2, and so on. Sometimes this can be handy, particularly if a selected "column" is actually a concatenation of several columns or a complex calculation. Rather than re-typing all of that, it can be a timesaver to just refer to it by its column numbering in the results, from left to right.

Using the ORDER BY number notation means that the SQL below is functionally equivalent to the SQL above:

```
SELECT title
    , page_count
    , publisher
    , first_edition_year
```

```
FROM books
ORDER BY 4 DESC;
```

While this is certainly handy, this notation is more susceptible to unpredictable ordering due to adding or deleting SELECT columns, or to reordering the columns. Having the actual column name in the ORDER BY clause ensures that the ordering of the result rows will not change even if the order of the SELECT columns changes.

# Where Did It All Go Wrong?

So you wrote some SQL and you followed all of the guidelines and it still does not run!  Where did it all go wrong?

The bad news is that a complete list of possible reasons is almost unlimited.  The good news is that the root causes can often be lumped into just a few general categories.  From there, it is usually not too difficult to pinpoint the exact issue.

### The SQL just doesn't run!  I get weird errors.

Did you copy the SQL from somewhere?  You may be the victim of invisible formatting characters that confuse your SQL client.  Try physically typing the SQL in your SQL client.  Another tactic would be to copy the SQL into a text editor – NOT a word processing program! – and then save it and copy that version into your client.  A good text editor will strip out excess formatting characters, giving you a clean, or at least cleaner, copy of the SQL.

### I get back too many rows!

This is the most common complaint.  Check your joins.  Often people concentrate so much on the WHERE conditions that they forget to join the tables!  This creates what is called a Cartesian Join.  In a Cartesian Join, every selected row in each table is joined with every other selected row in every other table in every possible combination. If your "simple" query returns pages and pages of rows, you probably have an issue with your joins.

### I get back multiple copies of some of the rows!

This might also be a join condition, so the joins should be checked first.  If that is not the issue, then it is entirely possible that the SQL correctly returns rows which look the same!  If all that you really want is a "representative" row (no duplicates), then insert the keyword DISTINCT after the SELECT statement and before the first column. This tells the database engine that you only want "one of each" selected row.

Suppose that you are trying to get a list of all of the books by a certain author. Your BOOKS table contains the fields, BOOK_ID, TITLE, PUBLISHER, FORMAT, and AUTHOR_ID. In this example, you know that the AUTHOR_ID = 1, so the SQL would be:

```
SELECT title
FROM books
WHERE author_id = 1;
```

Which returns:

```
TITLE
--------------------

My First Book
My First Book
My Second Book
My Second Book
```

What happened? Why did each title come up twice? The answer is that the uniqueness of the row is enforced by a primary key, in this case BOOK_ID, and that other fields in each row also make each row unique. This can be seen when selecting additional fields:

```
SELECT book_id
   , title
   , publisher
   , format as fmt
FROM books
WHERE author_id = 1;
```

```
   BOOK_ID TITLE                    PUBLISHER  FMT
---------- --------------------     ---------- ---
         1 My First Book            Lulu       HB
         2 My First Book            Lulu       LP
```

```
3 My Second Book        Lulu        HB
4 My Second Book        Lulu        PB
```

The PUBLISHER is the same, but the FORMAT (hardback [HB], paperback [PB], and large print [LP] if you are curious) and, of course, the primary key (BOOK_ID) are different.

Therefore, to just get a list of unique titles by an author, regardless of the other data fields, it is necessary to add DISTINCT to the SELECT clause:

```
SELECT DISTINCT title
FROM books
WHERE author_id = 1;

TITLE
--------------------
My First Book
My Second Book
```

Please remember to check your JOIN conditions first! It is much more costly to miss a JOIN condition and try to "fix" it with DISTINCT than it is to get the JOIN conditions correct and minimize the number of returned rows using DISTINCT.

**The database is not using all of my WHERE conditions!**

Rest assured that the SQL engine always uses all of the WHERE conditions. Consider that there may be a logical ambiguity as discussed with the OR keyword. If you verify that each individual condition is correct, then the issue may be with your data or, more precisely, your perception of your data. Sometimes the WHERE clause contains two or more conditions for the same table because "they always go together." Unless that truism is enforced by either the application or the database, that truism might be the culprit. Try removing WHERE conditions one at a time until the "missing" row suddenly appears. Keep in mind that several "other" rows might suddenly appear as well since you are removing conditions! When the "missing" row appears, you will need to figure out what it is about the latest condition that you removed caused that row to be excluded.

**NULLs**

In a database, a NULL value most often means that no value was entered for a field. This may seem pretty obvious, but there are great philosophical discussions surrounding, "What is NULL?" Seriously.

Keep the idea of NULL in mind if you run some SQL and the results do not exactly match what you expect. There might be a WHERE condition that eliminated one or more rows because a field was NULL. NULL is not zero! Zero is number representing the absence of something. NULL is the absence of a value. Therefore a "< 3" condition would find "0" but would not find a NULL as its value is unknown.

From a practical standpoint, NULL values probably exist in your database and you should be at least aware of their existence. The syntax with NULLs is also a little different in that you write:

```
<field> IS (NOT) NULL
```

rather than:

```
<field> = NULL
```

NULL values can sometimes cause some confusion. For instance, a table may contain a "Y/N" field, but a value is not required in that field, meaning that it can contain "blanks", or NULL values. If you were to separately count the number of rows in the table, the number of "Y" values, and the number of "N" values, then "Y count + N count" would not equal the number of rows in the table!

## Troubleshooting

If the problem does not become evident with about 15 minutes, get help! Finding workarounds generally leads to other issues and bad habits farther down the road. Kicking the same SQL over and over to try to bend it to your will just leads to frustration and, ultimately, does not get the job done. Better to ask for help. You might even learn something.

# Style

Style matters. I have worked with DBAs who would not even look at SQL that was not formatted to their satisfaction. I will admit that I am more favorably inclined to SQL that is formatted in a sensible fashion, even if it is not formatted in "my" style! Why? It is simply easier to read and comprehend a neatly formatted bit of SQL than it is to read a continuous, wrapped line of SQL, particularly when the SQL is long and joins many tables!

In a practical sense, formatting your SQL as a matter of habit can aid immensely with troubleshooting. The first thing I do when I get some "messy" SQL is to format it. More often than not, the problem almost jumps out at me!

What is a good style? Try to put each field, condition, table, etc. on a separate line, like this:

```
SELECT t1.col1
   , t1.col2
   , t2.col4
   , MIN(t2.col3) as minval
FROM table_one t1
   , table_two t2
WHERE t1.pk = t2.fk
   AND t1.col3 = 'SOME VALUE'
GROUP BY t1.col1
   , t1.col2
   , t2.col4
ORDER BY 4 DESC;
```

If the above SQL was just on a single line, it would look like:

```
SELECT t1.col1,t1.col2,t2.col4,MIN(t2.col3) as
minval FROM table_one t1,table_two t2 WHERE
t1.pk = t2.fk AND t1.col3 = 'SOME VALUE' GROUP
BY t1.col1,t1.col2,t2.col4 ORDER BY 4 DESC;
```

Which would you rather see?

There are also very practical reasons for putting your SQL on multiple lines. When the SQL contains an error, the database will often report which line it did not like. If everything is on "Line 1", that error message will not be particularly helpful to you. If the SQL is 25 lines and the database is unhappy with "Line 13", you have a very good starting point!

When running SQL, the easiest way to remove a line is to put a double dash (--) to the left of the line that you wish to exclude. This is similar to REM, #, or DOC in other languages, and indicates that the selected line is not to be used. Note that this might necessitate some additional reformatting to move a comma or an AND or some such. The normal syntax rules of SQL still apply! For example, if I wanted to exclude the t2.col4 field from the example above, it would look like:

```
SELECT t1.col1
   , t1.col2
--   , t2.col4
   , MIN(t2.col3) as minval
FROM table_one t1
   , table_two t2
WHERE t1.pk = t2.fk
  AND t1.col3 = 'SOME VALUE'
GROUP BY t1.col1
   , t1.col2
--   , t2.col4
--ORDER BY 4 DESC
ORDER BY 3 DESC;
```

Wait a minute! There are several things excluded now! Look at them individually and apply what you have learned. In the SELECT statement, the field is "removed" as desired. Because that row is removed, and there is an aggregate condition (MIN), that field should *probably* be removed from the GROUP BY clause as well. That field is not required to be removed from the GROUP BY clause, but most often the fields in the GROUP BY clause mirror the non-aggregated fields in the SELECT.

The ORDER BY actually has two changes! First, because a field was removed from the SELECT and the ORDER BY is done by position rather than by column name, there are only three fields rather than four. The second change is a little more subtle. Sometimes the SQL client will honor the semicolon even though the rest of the line has been "removed." In those cases, the "commented out" semicolon has to be removed as it may cause some confusion!

## Content vs. Format

Every database will return data looking exactly as it is stored in the database or with default formatting applied, as in the case of a DATE field. There are a great many options for formatting the data to get it just the way that you want it. Oracle has formatting commands available in SQL*Plus, the Oracle client. There are GUI tools in SQL Server Enterprise Manager that accomplish the same thing. If you are writing reports using a reporting tool such as Crystal Reports, the formatting options are almost limitless.

My point in all of this is that your biggest concern from the SQL side should be that you are retrieving the correct data. The formatting of the final results is, literally, just polishing the results to get a shine. The bulk of your efforts should be pointed towards getting the correct data!

# Odds and Ends

Remember that a SQL is just that, a query. A request. The more direct you can make your request, the better. If there is some part of your query that does not absolutely need to be there, then remove it! I have looked at many bits of SQL over the years and found "extra" tables or fields in the query. Perhaps at one time there was a field selected from the table. If that field is removed from the SELECT and the table is no longer necessary as part of the query, remove it. Likewise, sometimes "extra" fields are added to the SELECT "just in case" they might be needed. Add them when they are needed, and not before.

Build your SQL beginning with a single table and add as needed. Too often I receive a large query to troubleshoot and the SQL itself is just a disaster. Each time I run it I get an error. I correct that error only to get another error. More often than not, the SQL was written in one sitting as one amorphous mass of text. Those situations generally turn into a "Let's try this again" exercise, beginning with a single table, and others added as needed. It is much easier and less frustrating to build and iterate than it is to assemble a huge SQL worthy of the gods only to find that it has many issues, and often has to be rewritten from scratch.

The SQL engine for your database has been through the wars. Because of the nature of databases, the SQL engine has to return the same rows the same way from the same SQL every single time. Do not try to fight the database. You can yell at it. I do. Ultimately, though, the database needs to receive a SQL query that it can parse and execute. Understand that the path to learning involves getting in wrong from time to time. The important thing is to learn where you went wrong and try to correct it.

You will get better at SQL with practice. Keep practicing. Good luck!

www.ingramcontent.com/pod-product-compliance
Lightning Source LLC
Chambersburg PA
CBHW051217050326
40689CB00008B/1341